Goodnight '70s

Andrews McMeel Publishing
a division of Andrews McMeel Universal
1130 Walnut Street, Kansas City, Missouri 64106

www.andrewsmcmeel.com

All Photo Credits: Alamy Stock Photo

19 20 21 22 23 SHO 10 9 8 7 6 5 4 3 2 1

ISBN: 978-1-4494-9678-4

ATTENTION: SCHOOLS AND BUSINESSES
Andrews McMeel books are available at quantity discounts with
bulk purchase for educational, business, or sales promotional use.
For information, please e-mail the Andrews McMeel Publishing
Special Sales Department: specialsales@amuniversal.com.

Goodnight '70s

Peter Stein

Illustrated by Alyssa Bermudez

Andrews McMeel
PUBLISHING®

In the '70s room
There was
An 8-track tape
Playing a tune
And a disco ball—

4

5

As shiny as the moon

And cascading hair on a big beanbag chair

And tube socks and Pet Rocks

And a David Cassidy lunch box

And bell-bottom jeans on some tubular teens

And a cool game of Pong was played all day long

By a Happy Face smile

And a phone with a dial

13

While an unshowered Deadhead zoned out on the waterbed

The president was sneaking, a nude dude was streaking

And everybody was Kung Fu Fighting
By lava lamp lighting

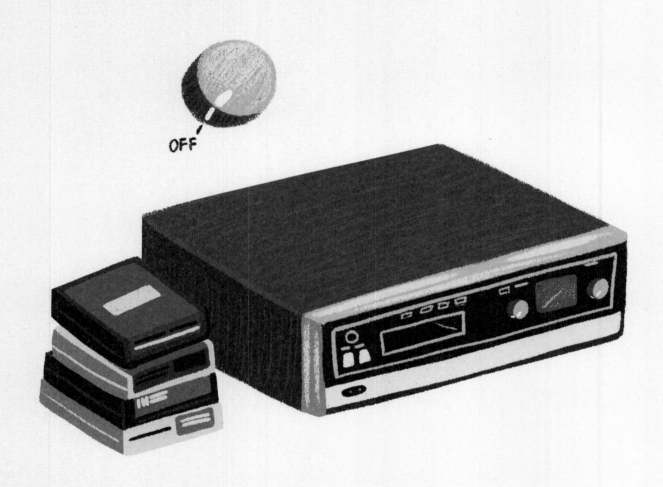

OFF

Goodnight tune

Goodnight disco ball as shiny as the moon

Goodnight long, groovy hair
Goodnight beanbag chair

Goodnight socks, rocks, and heartthrob lunch box

Goodnight flared jeans and righteous teens

Goodnight Pong, off all night long

Goodnight smile
And phone that took forever to dial

26

Goodnight Deadhead
Crashed on the waterbed

Goodnight Tricky Dick and nude dude so quick

Goodnight kung fu champs

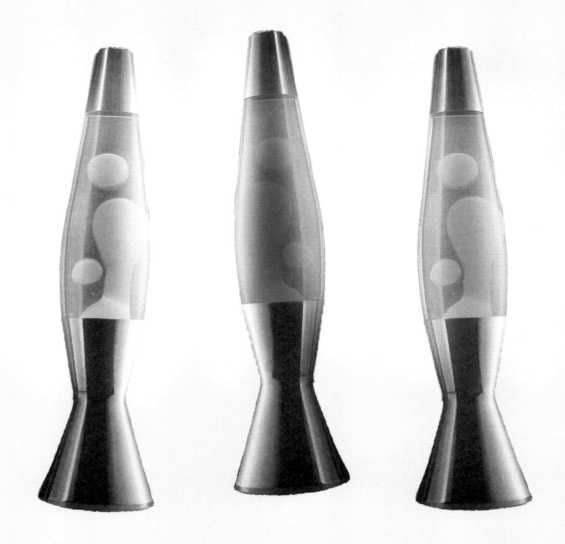

Goodnight lava lamps

GOODNIGHT '70s

There's really no doubt . . .

You were SUPER FAR OUT